The Rock Cycle
Road Trip

SOIL

Hit the road and discover a world that rocks!

CHERITON
CHILDREN'S BOOKS

Published in 2025 by **Cheriton Children's Books**
1 Bank Drive West, Shrewsbury, Shropshire, SY3 9DJ, UK

First Edition

Author: Sarah Eason
Designer: Paul Myerscough
Editor: Deborah Jones
Proofreader: Katie Dicker

Picture credits: Cover: Collaborate; Inside: p1: Shutterstock/Leka Leck, p4: Shutterstock/Lamyai, p5: Shutterstock/Withan Tor, p6: Shutterstock/Vadim Sadovski, p7: Shutterstock/Elena Arkadova, p8: Shutterstock/Sunny Forest, p9: Shutterstock/Nekomura, p10: Shutterstock/Smileus, p11: Shutterstock/Walshphotos, p12: Shutterstock/Mr Rawin Tanpin, p13: Shutterstock/Pixel-Shot, p14: Shutterstock/Akkharat Jarusilawong, p15: Wikimedia Commons/Sven Rosborn, p16b: Shutterstock/Galeh Kholis, p16t: Shutterstock/Petro Perutskyi, p18: Shutterstock/David Khelashvili, p19: Shutterstock/Erichon, p20b: Shutterstock/Vagonik, p20t: Shutterstock/Manfred Ruckszio, p21: Shutterstock/EyeTravel, p22: Shutterstock/Miks Mihails Ignats, p23b: Shutterstock/BlackMac, p23t: Shutterstock/Stephen James Burke, p24b: Shutterstock/Albert Frigole, p24t: Shutterstock/Natasa Re, p26: Shutterstock/Alexey Slyusarenko, p27: Shutterstock/Presslab, p28: Shutterstock/William Edge, p29: Shutterstock/D. Kucharski K. Kucharska, p30b: Shutterstock/Galyna Andrushko, p30t: Shutterstock/Hector Ruiz Villar, p31: Shutterstock/Zoltan Tarlacz, p32b: Shutterstock/Sirtravelalot, p32t: Shutterstock/Redknapper, p34: Shutterstock/JMx Images, p35: Shutterstock/Dmitry Fch, p36b: Shutterstock/Prapann, p36t: Shutterstock/Shamils, p38: Shutterstock/Fotofilia Maciej Pazera, p39: Shutterstock/Wirestock Creators, p40: Shutterstock/Everett Collection, p41: Shutterstock/Smit, p42b: Shutterstock/Elena Elisseeva, p43: Shutterstock/Komsan Loonprom.

Printed in China

Please visit our website,
www.cheritonchildrensbooks.com
to see more of our high-quality books.

CONTENTS

Chapter 1

Our Rocky World

Our planet is made almost entirely of rock. It has a small metal core at its center, but the remaining 85 percent of it is rock—and that's why it is so easy to find many amazing rocks on Earth.

All Change

Although the rocky surface of our planet may seem stable, it is being reshaped and reformed all the time. Sometimes, changes to its surface can happen quickly. For example, because of a natural disaster such as a landslide or earthquake. Most of the time, the changes to Earth's rocky surface happen very, very slowly—so slowly that we hardly notice them. Over a very long period, surface rocks are broken down to make way for new rocks. This is part of a never-ending cycle called the rock cycle.

Earth's Rock Cycle

The rock cycle is a process by which one type of rock changes into another type of rock. Earth has three main types of rock: igneous rock, metamorphic rock, and sedimentary rock. Each can change into another type when affected by temperature, **weathering**, and **pressure**.

As rocks break down, they also create soil. Read on to find out more!

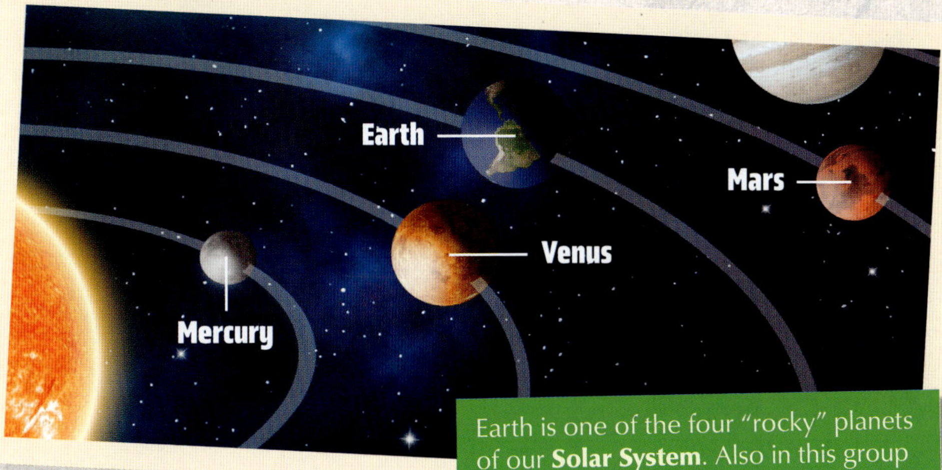

Earth is one of the four "rocky" planets of our **Solar System**. Also in this group are Mercury, Venus, and Mars.

How Rock Changes

When heated deep underground, rocks turn into liquid rock. We call this melted rock magma. When rocks are worn away by weathering or erosion, they break into smaller pieces called sediment. Rock can also be squeezed under great pressure, which also forces it to change.

Understanding Rock Types

READ *Here*

Igneous rock is magma that has cooled and hardened. This can happen above or below the ground. Igneous rock changes by melting into magma, eroding into sediment, or being pressed so tightly that it becomes metamorphic rock.

Metamorphic rock began life as igneous or sedimentary rock that was then heated and squeezed. Metamorphic rock can change again by eroding into sediment or melting into magma.

Sedimentary rock is made up of squashed sediments from other rocks, plus the remains of living things. It can erode back into sediment, be squeezed into metamorphic rock, or melted into magma.

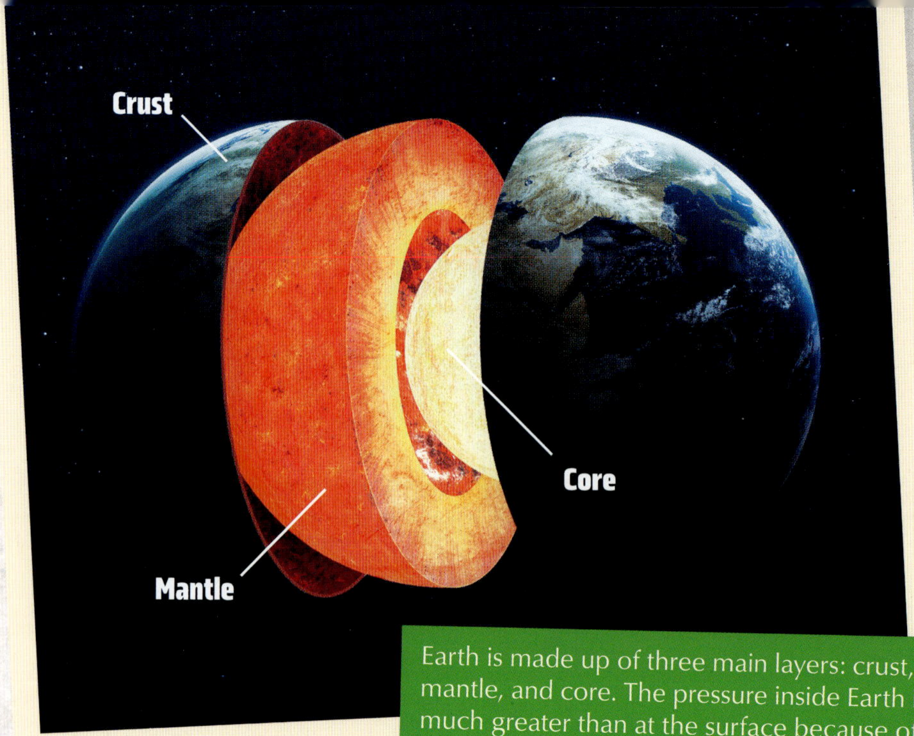

Earth is made up of three main layers: crust, mantle, and core. The pressure inside Earth is much greater than at the surface because of the downward push of millions of tons of rock above.

Look Inside Earth

To understand the rock cycle and why rock is so affected by temperature, weathering, and pressure, we need to first look at the structure of Earth.

Earth looks solid and immovable at the surface, but inside are layers that are not at all like the surface. In fact, Earth is made up of three very different parts.

Crust: This is the outer part of our planet. It is the section on which we live. It is up to 44 miles (70 km) thick and is broken up into enormous parts, called plates.

Mantle: This mostly solid layer moves around and is about 1,800 miles (2,900 km) thick. Earth's plates float on the mantle.

Core: This is the hottest part of our planet and it forms the center of Earth. The center of the core reaches nearly 12,000 degrees Fahrenheit (6,700 °C), hot enough to keep it permanently molten, or liquid.

Rock Recycling

During the rock cycle, new rock material can rise to the surface from deep within Earth. But most surface rocks are made from existing rock that is continually recycled. For example, as a rock is weathered, a grain within it may be loosened. That grain may then become part of another rock. It will then be weathered and separated from that rock, then form part of a new rock, repeatedly. Soil isn't a rock, but it's an important part of the rock cycle. Soil forms from the breakdown of surface rocks by weather and is an amazing **resource** that all living things depend on.

Take a Rock Cycle Road Trip!

In this book, we will explore how soil is created, the different types of soil that exist, and why they are so useful to us. We'll take an amazing rock cycle road trip to discover soil around the world, the living things that help keep soil healthy, and why soil is so important to us. So, what are you waiting for? Let's hit the road and discover a world that rocks!

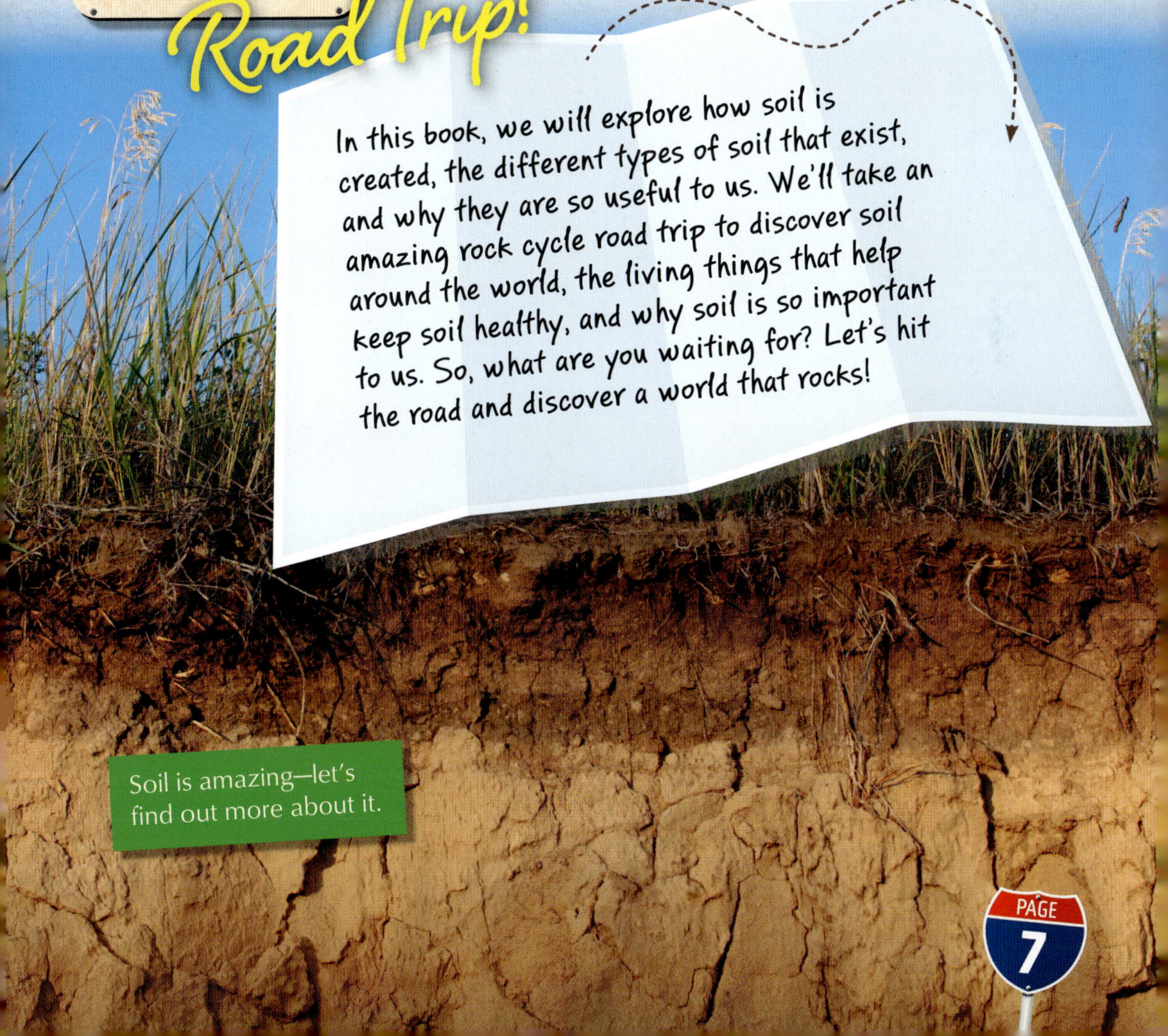

Soil is amazing—let's find out more about it.

A Living System

Most people do not think about the soil beneath their feet. They walk around on it, play sport on it, maybe even dig and grow plants in it, but they do not stop to think about the secrets in the soil. Many people think soil is just dirt, but soil is far more than that—it is a living system.

We depend on soil for our food.

Full of Life

The layer of earth that covers much of our land is made up of a huge variety of things. They include pieces of rock that may have been formed by volcanoes, decaying plants and animals and their waste, air, water, and millions of living things.

Can't Live Without It!

Almost everything that we need can be traced back to soil, from food, clothing, and paper to wood and even the air we breathe. We depend on soil to grow food and to hold up our buildings. Soil is an amazing resource and our lives would not be the same without it.

Not a Lot of Soil

Although soil is one of the most important resources on Earth, there isn't a lot of soil to go around. Earth's land surface covers 57 million square miles (148 million sq km). Of that area, **deserts** and **ice sheets** make up 31 percent of land and forests another 31 percent. The 38 percent left is agricultural land, or land that can be used for farming, and only about one-third of that land can be used to grow food or fiber for textiles.

Digging Deeper

Soil never stays still—it is constantly changing. There are four main ways that soil changes. Things can be added to soil, for example, rain adds water to soil and dust can add **minerals** to soil. Things can be taken away from soil, for example, water can wash soil particles away. Soil moves—gravity can pull soil down and animals in the soil can make it move around. Parts of soil can also change, for example, wind and rain can break down hard rocks in soil into smaller pieces.

READ Here

Much of Earth's surface is covered in land that cannot be farmed, such as ice sheets or deserts. That is why our precious farmland, with its rich soil, is so important to us.

Chapter 2

The Story of Soil

Soil includes air, water, minerals, and a material called humus, which is made up of decaying dead plants and animals. Half of soil is made up of air and water. The mineral part of soil includes tiny grains of rock. However, the rocks we see around us range from beach pebbles to cliff faces and high mountains. So, how do the grains of rock in soil get to be so small?

Broken Down

The rocks on Earth's surface are constantly being broken down by wind, water, and ice. This is called weathering. Wind can toss grains of sand against a rock and wear away the surface. Rushing water in a river can scrape boulders across a rock's surface and break off chunks. Rainwater contains acids that can wear away rock, too. Sea stacks are vertical columns of rock found along rocky coasts. They are the result of ocean forces. Waves gradually change a small crack in a chunk of **protruding** rock into an arch. Eventually, the arch roof becomes so thin it collapses, leaving a separate stack standing in the ocean.

Soil is created over a long period of time. In fact, it can take up to 1,000 years to make just a couple of inches (5 cm) of soil.

Sea stacks are a very visible form of the weathering effect of water on rock.

Digging Deeper

Scientists who study soil are known as soil pedologists and soil morphologists. They examine soil to find out how it formed, how soil can best be managed by humans, and what impact people have on soil and how it changes. People also map soils to show what type of soils exist in different areas.

READ Here

No Rock Too Hard

Weathering can turn even very hard rocks, such as granite, to dust. If water gets into a tiny crack in the rock and then expands as it turns into ice, it forces the crack to open. When this happens again and again, the crack grows bigger and bigger, until the rock splits. The smaller pieces of rock then break down further to create soil.

The Layers of Soil

All soil is made up of four main layers, but the depth and ingredients in each layer can vary. Topsoil is the upper layer and is made up of minerals and living and rotting materials such as leaves, plants, and worms. It contains a lot of humus so it usually looks dark. Subsoil is the next layer and contains less **organic matter** than topsoil but more minerals. It is usually lighter in color, too. Next up is weathered rock. This layer is made up of small pieces of rock and a very small quantity of organic matter. Last of all is bedrock, which is a solid layer of rock that forms the base or bed of the soil.

This illustration shows the four main layers of soil.

Different Types of Soil

Soils have similar basic ingredients, but there are many different types of soil. Scientists have identified more than 70,000 types of soil in the United States alone. Soils look different depending on their makeup. Red soils contain more iron minerals and dark soils are rich in humus. Soils that contain harder minerals may have larger rock grains and contain more gravel. Clay minerals soak up water, so clay soils feel stickier.

Soils can be black, brown, gray, red, or yellow. They can be crumbly, soft, or grainy.

Digging Deeper

Did you know that soils have parents?! They **inherit** characteristics from the parent material from which they formed. For example, soils that formed from limestone rock have a lot of calcium and soils that formed from materials at the bottom of lakes have a lot of clay.

The Soil Stars

There are many, many different types of soil on Earth. Some of the best known are sandy, loam, clay, silt, chalk, peat, and volcanic.

Describing Soil

Soil is often described using characteristics such as texture, temperature, and color. One of the most important characteristics of soil is its texture. That is because the texture of soil tells us how much water is in the soil. For example, a sandy texture is typical of soil that does not hold a lot of water. A clay texture is a characteristic of soil that does hold a lot of water.

Soil Around the World

There are many different types of soil around the world. They range from the dry sandy soils of hot deserts to the frozen permafrost soils of the far north. The climate of a region is an important factor in the types of soil found there.

Woolly mammoths have been found perfectly preserved in Siberian permafrost, as though stored in a deep freeze. Even their hair remained! Without finds like these, we would not be able to accurately create models of long-dead species.

Soil in Hot Places

Desert soils are shallow and dry because they form in **arid** climates. Soil formation is usually limited to near the surface. Water does not move through the soil and the lack of water means there are few plants.

Soil in Cold or Rainy Places

Around the Poles and on high mountains, the subsoil can remain permanently frozen and is known as permafrost. In warm regions that get plenty of rain, organic matter rots more quickly and deeply, so rich soils can form.

Digging Deeper

The contents of an area of soil tell us a lot about its history. Soil can reveal what the weather was like in the past, what animals and plants lived and grew in an area, and how much water covered the land long ago.

READ Here

Take a

Rock Cycle Road Trip!

Human remains have also been preserved in certain soils for thousands of years. Boggy soils contain few **decomposers** to rot a body, and one Danish bog revealed the body of a man who had died 2,500 years ago! It's the first stop on our road trip.

SOIL STOP! BJAELDSKOVDAL BOG, EUROPE

In 1950, two Danish brothers named Viggo and Emil Højgaard were digging peat in Bjaeldskovdal bog when their shovels hit the body of a man. His body was amazingly well preserved—even the belt and cap he was wearing had survived. A leather thong was also wrapped around his neck, showing that he had been strangled to death. He was named the Tollund Man.

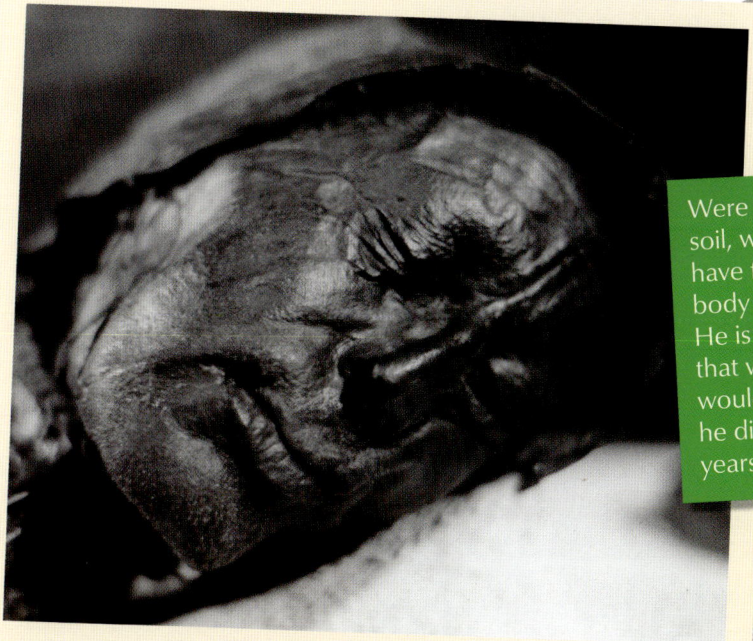

Were it not for boggy soil, we would not have found the preserved body of the Tollund Man. He is so well preserved that we can see how he would have looked when he died thousands of years ago.

PEAT

What a Soil Star!

Peat soil is found in **wetland** areas that include bogs, fens, swamps, and marshes. More than half of the wetlands on Earth have peat soil. In fact, peatland covers about 3 percent of the land and freshwater surface of Earth.

THAT ROCKS!

Peat soil is great for the environment because it traps twice as much **carbon** as all the world's forests combined! However, digging up peat is not so good for the environment because in doing so, the carbon the peat contains is released.

Soil Star Characteristics

- Contains a lot of water
- Soft and spongy texture
- Contains few decomposers

Peat is found in wetland areas around the world. It is more common in the northern part of the planet. However, it is also found in **humid** and tropical parts of Southeast Asia, such as around mangrove swamps.

Take a

Rock Cycle *Road Trip!*

Peat Hotspots

Other great places to find peat soil are:

Did You Know?

The lack of oxygen in peat is one reason why plants and animals do not completely decay in it. Certain **bacteria** break down matter, such as the bodies of dead plants and animals, but these bacteria rely on oxygen to survive. With its lack of oxygen, peat is not a good environment for the bacteria. The cooler temperatures and acidic water of many peat bogs also help dead plants and animals to stay well preserved.

Grains of rock can be washed to new areas by heavy rainstorms or floods.

Mysterious Rock

In some cases, soil develops directly from the rock that lies beneath it. Often, however, a mysterious mix of different rock types is found in soil. Sometimes, soil contains grains from a type of rock that is not found anywhere near it—so, how does this happen?

A Long-Distance Mover

The grains of rock that form soils can be moved enormous distances. Erosion is a process in which pieces of rock that have been worn away by weathering are carried to new places. Small pieces of lightweight rock can be blown a long way by winds. You can see this happening if you stand on a beach on a windy day and watch the grains of sand being blown by the wind.

A Force of Nature

Water is a very powerful force of nature. Rivers can cross **continents** and carry rocks extremely long distances. Fast-flowing rivers can transport large rocks, but slow-moving rivers mainly transport tiny pieces of rock.

Take a

Rock Cycle Road Trip!

Rivers are very important to farmers. Not only do they carry grains of rock that make up soil, but they also carry water and important **nutrients** to the surrounding soil. That helps crops grow. One of the best examples of this can be seen in the farmland surrounding the Nile River, in Africa—and it's the next stop on our road trip. Head this way!

SOIL STOP! THE NILE RIVER, AFRICA

A lot of the soil around the Nile River is silt, which contains important minerals. Volcanic **eruptions** in the **uplands** of Egypt **deposited** rich minerals on the surrounding land, which were then picked up by the Nile River as it flowed through the uplands. The mineral-containing silt was then deposited on the land further downstream, before the river eventually emptied into the Mediterranean Sea.

Silt is a great soil for growing crops because it holds on to water well. Silt also holds on to nutrients, which feed plants. That is why the land around the Nile River is so great for farming.

The Nile River has naturally irrigated, or watered, the land around its shores for thousands of years. The river snakes through Egypt, making its way toward the Mediterranean Sea.

SILT

What a Soil Star!

Silt is formed when larger rocks such as quartz and feldspar are eroded by wind and water. The pieces of rock are carried along by **glaciers**, flowing water, and wind. As they travel, the pieces grind against each other, which further wears them down. Eventually, they form a dustlike material—silt.

Soil Star Characteristics

- Feels smooth when wet and is floury in texture
- Feels slippery or greasy when wet
- Keeps hold of water

Many frogs and toads **hibernate** in soil to keep warm through the winter months.

THAT ROCKS!

Silt provides a warm home for some frogs during cold winter months. The animals bury themselves in the soft layer of silt at the bottom of lakes and ponds. The water at the bottom does not freeze and the silt makes a cozy covering for the frogs that hide in it.

Take a

Rock Cycle Road Trip!

Did You Know?

Silt is made up of rock and mineral pieces that are so small they are hard to see. A silt particle can be less than .002 inches (.005 cm) across. Soil is classed as silt if 80 percent of it, or more, is made up of silt particles.

Silt Hotspots

Other great places to find silt soil are:

About 60 percent of the soil around the Mississippi River **delta** is silt.

Slow Beginnings, Dramatic Starts

Most soils take hundreds of years to form, or even longer, but some have more dramatic beginnings. They form suddenly following landslides, volcanoes, or heavy storms.

Fast-Moving Earth

A landslide or mudflow is an event in which a lot of sediment moves suddenly downhill. This often happens after rainstorms. Mountains have sloping sides, so when the loose rock and soil on the sides become wet and heavy, they can suddenly become unstable. They can build up a lot of speed, run off the mountain slope, and form a layer of soil in a new area of flat land below.

Explosive Changes

A volcanic eruption can change the soil in an area dramatically. When a volcano erupts, it rains volcanic ash down onto Earth's surface. This ash mixes with other grains of rock to form a rich, dark soil.

Landslides can result in the movement of huge amounts of earth.

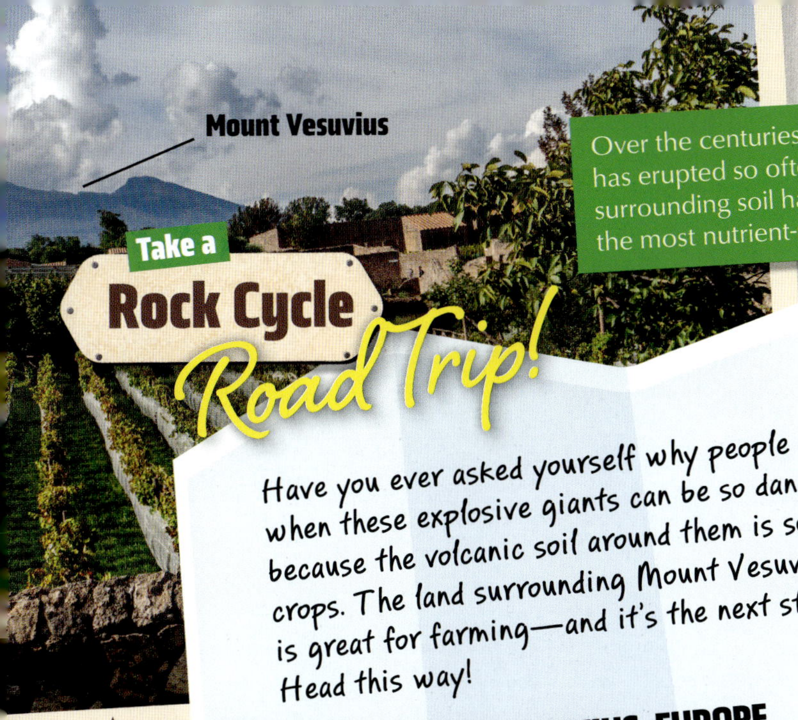

Over the centuries, Mount Vesuvius has erupted so often that the surrounding soil has become one of the most nutrient-rich soils in the world.

Take a Rock Cycle Road Trip!

Have you ever asked yourself why people live near volcanoes when these explosive giants can be so dangerous? It is because the volcanic soil around them is so good for growing crops. The land surrounding Mount Vesuvius in Italy, Europe, is great for farming—and it's the next stop on our road trip. Head this way!

SOIL STOP! MOUNT VESUVIUS, EUROPE

Volcanic ash is rich in nutrients that plants take in through their roots to help them grow, which is why the soil surrounding one of Italy's most famous volcanoes is rich farmland. The soil is sandy and rich in minerals such as iron, potassium, phosphorus, and silica.

The area around the volcano also attracted people in ancient times—the Romans. They built the nearby town of Pompeii and settled around the volcano, using its rich soil to grow many crops, including wheat, barley, olives, and fruits.

The rich volcanic soil provided the people of Pompeii with a steady supply of crops, until the volcano erupted in a giant explosion in 79 CE, destroying the town and killing thousands of its people.

When Vesuvius erupted, the volcanic ash helped preserve some of the bodies of the residents of Pompeii, which can still be seen today.

VOLCANIC SOIL

What a Soil Star!

Volcanic soil belongs to a group of soils known as andisols. These soils contain volcanic lava and volcanic ash. Both are rich in important nutrients, such as iron, calcium, magnesium, and sulfur. All these nutrients help plants grow, which is why volcanic soil is perfect for farming.

Soil Star Characteristics

- Often very dark in color
- Has a glassy and spongy texture
- Holds on to water well

Did You Know?

When ash is thrown from a volcano, it can travel even farther than lava—sometimes for many, many miles. Initially, the ash is harmful, covering everything in a stifling blanket. However, a lot of volcanic ash quickly becomes mixed with soil, adding important nutrients to it and encouraging plant life to grow and thrive once more.

Take a

Rock Cycle Road Trip!

Volcanic Soil Hotspots

Other great places to find volcanic soil are:

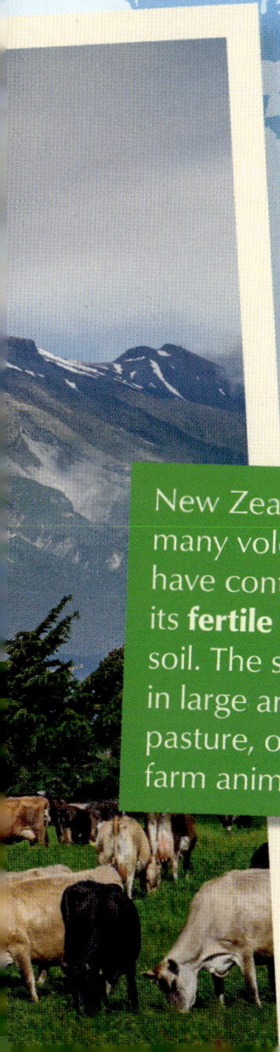

New Zealand has many volcanoes that have contributed to its **fertile** farmland soil. The soil results in large areas of rich pasture, on which farm animals graze.

THAT ROCKS!

When a volcano erupts, it may throw out lava, gases, and ash. Lava can ooze for miles around a volcano, forming an area called a lava field. Once the lava begins to harden it can be broken down into tiny pieces by rain and wind, over many years, eventually forming nutrient-rich soil.

Chapter 3

Living in Soil

As well as growing in soil, plants play an important role in the general composition and makeup of soil. In fact, plants make soil a living, breathing thing!

Breaking Down and Building Up

When plants grow in soil, their roots stretch between and around the grains of rock in it. The plant uses its roots to anchor itself in the ground so it can stand tall. However, acids released by the roots of some plants break down the rock on which the soil is forming. Roots also help bind the grains of rock together in newly formed soil. As the roots grow and tunnel through the soil, they open spaces to let in the air and water that make up the soil.

Plant and tree roots reach down and out into soil, making spaces for air and water and pushing into rock to break it up.

Soil scientists add **chemicals** to soil to see what effect they have on the soil and the plants that grow in it.

Digging Deeper

Scientists who study soil spend a lot of time examining it to find out what impact human activity is having on soil. Soil chemists study soil to discover how a chemical leak can affect surrounding soil. They will try to find out how the chemical moves within soil, and how quickly. They will also try to learn how quickly the chemical breaks down. Today, more chemicals are being leaked into soil than ever in our history. That is because of pollution, farming activities that use chemicals, and industrial waste that makes its way into waterways.

READ Here

Food Factories

Plants are amazing. They are the only living things that make their own food using the power of sunlight. They use **carbon dioxide** from the air and water from the soil to make sugars that help them grow stems, leaves, flowers, fruits, and seeds. When plant parts drop off and plants die, they decay and release their stored nutrients into the soil, enriching the soil itself.

Soil Supporter

Plants can even help break up rocks into smaller grains that make up soil. When plants start to grow in a crack in a rock, their roots widen the crack as they expand and spread, eventually breaking the rock apart.

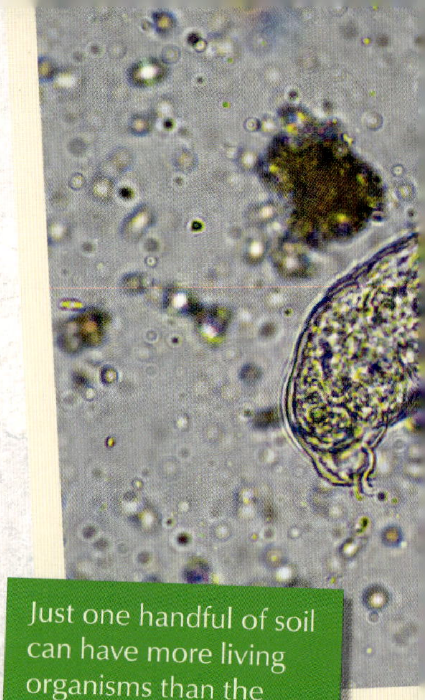

Little Things, Big Job

Many of the organisms in soil are so small that we can only see them with a microscope, but they do a big job. These **microorganisms** are nature's recyclers. They break down plant and animal waste into substances that help make soil the incredibly useful resource that it is.

Tiny Powerhouses

Living microorganisms, such as bacteria, tiny creatures called mites, and fungi such as mushrooms, are a vital ingredient of soil. These decomposers feed on organic waste, such as leaves and animal dung. As they do so, they release nutrients into the soil that form humus. Humus helps bind tiny grains of rock together and helps soil store water.

Just one handful of soil can have more living organisms than the people on Earth! In fact, less than half an ounce (1 g) of healthy soil can hold up to 1 billion bacteria.

Different Bacteria

Most of the bacteria in soil need oxygen to survive. They are called aerobic bacteria. Other bacteria can survive without oxygen, and some types can live both with and without oxygen. How quickly and well bacteria grow in soil depends on how oxygen-rich it is and the amount of nutrients.

Digging Deeper

Not all bacteria and fungi are helpful. Scientists studying soil discovered that the Great Potato Famine in Ireland, Europe, in the 1840s was caused by a fungus that created a disease caused potato blight. The disease destroyed potato crops and left much of Ireland's population starving, because they relied on the potatoes as food.

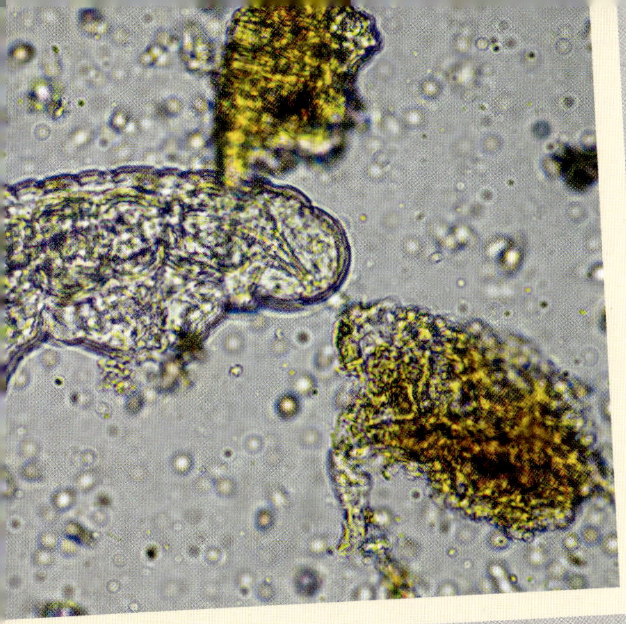

Flower Power

Flowering plants make tiny pollen grains that help them make seeds. In some soils, the tough outer coating of a pollen grain can survive long after the plant has rotted away. Scientists can examine the pollen in these soils to discover when it was alive and what type of plant grew there at that time.

A Team of Tunnelers

Earthworms bring organic matter down from the topsoil and mix it with the soil below. Their tunnels let in air and water that bacteria and other microorganisms need to survive. Earthworms also make soil **fertilizer**. They eat soil and as it passes out of their body, it forms worm-shaped coils of dirt called casts. These casts contain important soil nutrients.

Earthworms are soil heroes!

Moles were made for digging—and that helps soil!

Animals Are a Soil's Best Friend

Many larger animals live in soil, too. Prairie dogs, badgers, mice, and other animals find shelter underground or feed on roots or smaller animals in soil. They also help create soil and keep it healthy.

Animal Army

Ants, rabbits, prairie dogs, and many other animals dig burrows into soil. Moles have shovel-shaped front feet with tough, wide claws to help them dig efficiently. As these animals dig their tunnels, they loosen and mix the soil. This helps spread organic matter and minerals throughout the soil. It also lets in more air and water.

The Wonder of Waste

Waste, including feces, from animals and their activities add nutrients to the soil. For example, mice carry seeds and other plant materials into their underground burrows, into food stores, and to make bedding. This material gradually decays and becomes part of the soil.

Prairie soil is ideal for growing plants that provide us with important grains such as oats and wheat. They are used to make many foods that we eat, from cereals to bread.

Take a

Rock Cycle Road Trip!

Prairie dogs dig huge networks of tunnels in soil. These helpful creatures are found in the prairies of North America, which is the next stop on our road trip. Head this way!

SOIL STOP! THE AMERICAN PRAIRIES, NORTH AMERICA

The prairie grassland soil of North America is perfect for growing grains such as maize, wheat, rye, and oats. Farmers mainly grow maize, potatoes, soybeans, alfalfa, and cotton in prairie areas. Prairie dogs are often accused of damaging farm machinery or injuring cattle because of their burrows, and are blamed for eating and damaging crops. But these furry critters are also soil heroes!

Prairie dogs dig enormous systems of tunnels, with many different chambers. They have chambers where babies are kept, for sleeping, and even for toilets! As well as making burrows that let in air and mix soil, prairie dogs eat a lot of plants. This stops the surface from becoming overgrown and allows a variety of plants to thrive. As a result, a wider range of nutrients from prairie dog waste is added to the soil.

Prairie dog tunnels are designed to let air flow through, which is why they are so good for soil.

LOAM

What a Soil Star!

Loam soil is often described as the perfect soil for farmers and gardeners because it is ideal for growing plants. The soil usually has more nutrients, water, and humus than sandy soils. It also drains water more effectively than silt or clay soils. Loam soil is also easier to dig and plow than heavy clay soils.

California has a lot of loam soil. The region is famous for its vineyards, with rows of grapevines that thrive in the soil.

Soil Star Characteristics

- Often quite dark in color
- Often has a smooth or silky texture
- Feels soft and crumbly

THAT ROCKS!

Since ancient times, people have used loam soil to make bricks. The soil is mixed with water, sand, and mud. Straw or rice husks are added to bind the materials. The brick is then left to dry in the Sun and warm air.

Take a Rock Cycle Road Trip!

Loam Hotspots

Great places to find loam soil are warmer parts of the world, including:

Did You Know?

Loam soil is one of the most fertile of soils because it has the perfect combination of sand, clay, and silt particles. That means the soil holds on to water but also allows good drainage. For that reason, loam soil does not dry out in summer or become waterlogged in winter.

Chapter 4

Soil—We Need It!

Living things depend on soil. There are more than 10,000 types of plants on Earth that we can eat, and they all need soil for their own nutrients and water. Animals rely on plants for their food, and we need animals for food, too. Soil is precious to us, but we are harming it.

Farming as a Foe

Overusing or mistreating soils can ruin them. When people cut down all the trees in an area, there are no roots to hold the soil together. The wind and rain can blow and wash the valuable topsoil away.

Water and Chemical Problems

People also spoil soil when they remove too much water from below ground, for factories or other uses. This leaves the soil dry. In some places, heavy machinery can compact soil. This reduces the space available for air and water that the living things in soil, and therefore the soil itself, need to survive. Overuse of artificial **insecticides** and other farm sprays can also lower the number of decomposers in the soil, which reduces the number of nutrients and humus in it.

Overfarming leaves soil damaged and unusable. It is hoped that new farming methods will make crop growing easier for farmers of the future.

When too many farm animals graze an area for a long time, they strip it of its plant cover and loss of topsoil results.

Take a Rock Cycle Road Trip!

Some parts of the world have very poor soil today. Areas of Sub-Saharan Africa have very old soil that has been farmed for a long, long time—this continent is the final stop on our road trip.

SOIL STOP! SUB-SAHARAN AFRICA

The soil in parts of Sub-Saharan Africa has few nutrients left. Weather and unsustainable farming have made much of the soil unsuitable for crop growing. Today, food can only be grown on it with the help of fertilizers and irrigation. If people cannot afford fertilizers and do not have access to enough water, their plant crops die, which can lead to famine.

Projects encouraging farmers to grow crops more sustainably are now underway in Africa. Sustainable farming practices include growing a more diverse range of crops, and rotating crops. Planting trees among crops to provide shade and help improve the soil structure are other forms of sustainable farming.

SAND

What a Soil Star!

Sandy soils contain a lot of sand particles, and few clay particles. That makes the soil light and easy to work with. However, the soil is often low in nutrients.

THAT ROCKS!

Sandy soil has the largest soil particles of all soil types, with large air spaces between the particles. The large air spaces mean the soil contains plenty of oxygen. Sand particles are mainly made up of limestone, shale, granite, and quartz rock.

Soil Star Characteristics

- Often quite light in color
- Often has a dry texture
- Easy to rub between the fingers

Sandy soil is often found in southern and western Australia. In these areas, farmers are focusing on improved farming techniques to make sure the soil is not damaged by overgrazing and other issues. Some plants, such as cacti, which do not require a lot of water, also thrive in sandy soil.

Take a Rock Cycle Road Trip!

Did You Know?

Sandy soil is known as light soil because it contains so much sand and little clay, which weighs more than sand. The soil tends to warm up quickly in spring, because it is naturally dry, but can also dry out quickly during times of little rainfall. Adding organic matter to sandy soil can increase the nutrients in it and help the soil hold on to water more effectively.

Sandy Soil Hotspots

Sandy soil is found around the edge of the world's continents, and also in the middle of continents, in deserts and other dry areas such as:

Soil—What a Star!

You will be amazed by all the things soil does for us. We use soil with clay particles in it to make bricks for buildings. We need soil to grow plants, and we use plants in countless ways. Plants provide us with food, from fruit juices to the wheat that makes pizza dough, and provides food to feed the animals we eat.

Fuel, Furniture, and Clean Air

We cut down trees and use the wood for fuel, furniture, building, and even making paper. Plants also make the air healthier. Plants clean our air by taking out carbon dioxide and converting it to oxygen, which animals need to breathe. Without soil, none of this would be possible.

Bare Without Soil

Without soil, water would run onto bare rocks! When it rains, soil acts a little like a sponge—it soaks up water that runs onto the ground. Then, that water is used by plants and other living things in the soil. The water also moves into underground water stores, lakes, streams, and rivers, before eventually reaching the oceans.

We rely on soil to clean and store Earth's precious water.

All the things in an **ecosystem** depend on one another for survival, and without soil, many ecosystems could not exist.

Cleaning and Storing

Rainfall often contains pollution. Soil acts like a filter to remove pollutants, which are captured by soil particles. That cleans the water before it makes its way into waterways. Soil also collects and stores a lot of the water that we need for drinking, washing, cleaning, and cooking.

Link in the Chain

Soil provides a link between air, water, rocks, and living things. It is an important part of complex, vital systems in the natural world that we call ecosystems. Ecosystems are made up of plants, animals, and the things they need to survive such as air, water, soil, and sunlight.

Digging Deeper

Without soil, we would live in a world of waste! Waste buried in landfill sites is broken down by the decomposers that live in soil. Unfortunately, plastic, glass, metal, and other nonorganic waste cannot be broken down like this. That is why it is best to reuse or recycle these kinds of waste if you can.

READ *Here*

Saving Soil

Soil is a vital resource for us and our planet, but it takes about 500 years to develop just half a teaspoon of rich soil that is suitable for growing plants. That is why it is important to protect and preserve soil.

Stopping Erosion

To stop the precious layer of topsoil from becoming dry and washing or blowing away, people often add new plants to it. For example, trees and plants stop wind from reaching the soil and plant roots bind the soil together. When there are more plants, more water soaks into the soil, helping to keep it moist.

Digging Deeper

We have learned lessons from history about overfarming and the damage it can do to soil. After World War I (1914–1918), farmers in the United States tried to grow more crops than ever to supply people with food. They cleared large areas of grassland to make way for crops, and continually planted and harvested them, without allowing the soil to rest.

In the 1930s, terrible **droughts** hit. Crops failed and died. When the plants died, the overplowed topsoil was exposed. The soil had become dry and dusty from lack of rain, and without plant roots to hold it together, it easily blew away in the wind.

Terrible dust storms in the 1930s were caused by overfarming. Farmland was devastated, and growing crops became extremely difficult. This time of drought, and the area in which it occurred, became known as The Dust Bowl.

Soil can be described as the digestive system of our planet—it is constantly consuming, digesting, and recycling nutrients and organisms.

A New Way of Farming

Today, more and more farmers are working in ways that keep soil healthy. For example, they are using fewer artificial chemicals on their fields, which increases the number of decomposers in the soil. They are growing plants that attract insects and other animals that eat crop pests, so they do not have to use as many insecticides. They are reducing the number of times they plow a field in a year, which stops the soil from becoming compacted. By caring for the soil, farmers are helping ensure that it will provide food for many years to come, and the more we all do to help protect our planet's precious soil, the more we can preserve it for the future.

The Road Trip *Guide to* Soil Hunting

Had a great road trip? Loved the book? Want to try out soil hunting yourself? Awesome! Here's an easy guide that will explain the basics. The great thing about searching for soil is that anyone can do it and it costs very little. All you need is a pair of sharp eyes and some resources such as books and websites to help you identify the soil. A few key pieces of kit help too.

Tools include gloves, a trowel, and a magnifying glass, so you can examine soil in detail.

Collecting Soil Samples

The soil hunter's most important tools are a small shovel or trowel and something to collect soil in, such as a small pail or some grocery bags. You only need to collect a small sample of soil to analyze it.

A notebook or a smartphone camera is also useful, for recording your finds.

SOIL CLUES

Use these questions to help you identify common soils. The best way to tell what type of soil you have is by touching it and rolling it in your hands.

- Sandy soil is gritty—you can feel sand grains within it, and it falls through your fingers. It cannot be rolled to make a sausage shape. If it is not a coarse sand and perhaps a mixture of sand and loam, it may stick together better.
- Clay soil smears when you rub it on paper or cloth, and is sticky when wet. It is easily rolled into a long, thin sausage and can be smoothed to a shiny finish by rubbing with a finger. If it is not a heavy clay, it won't get quite as shiny and will not be as easy to make a sausage.
- Pure silt soils are rare, especially in gardens and backyards. They have a slightly soapy, slippery texture, and do not clump easily.

The Rock Cycle Road Trip QUIZ

How much have you learned about soil, the rock cycle, and our amazing planet on your road trip? Take the quiz and find out!

1. What is humus made up of?

2. What is weathering?

3. What are the four main layers of soil?

4. What main characteristic is used to describe soil?

5. Why does a lack of oxygen in peat soil help preserve living things?

6. Why is silt soil good for farming?

7. What is the benefit of living near a volcano?

8. Why do animals help soil?

9. What soil type is best for gardeners?

10. Name one way we can stop soil erosion.

ANSWERS

1. Decaying dead plants and animals
2. The process by which rock is broken down into tiny grains by wind, water, or ice
3. Topsoil, subsoil, weathered rock, bedrock
4. Texture
5. Because some of the bacteria that break down dead matter need oxygen to survive
6. It contains many nutrients and holds on to water well
7. The surrounding soil is good for farming
8. They dig holes in soil which mixes and loosens the soil and lets air and water in. They also help fertilize soil with their waste
9. Loam because it is ideal for growing plants—it is full of nutrients, holds and drains water well, and is easy to dig
10. By planting trees and plants in soil

GLOSSARY

arid a climate or area of dry land with little rain, making it difficult for plants to grow

bacteria tiny single-celled organisms that are found almost everywhere on Earth and are vital to the planet's ecosystems

carbon an important chemical element that combines with other elements to make compounds. Carbon compounds make up about one-fifth of the matter in living things

carbon dioxide a colorless, odorless gas found naturally in air. Animals breathe out carbon dioxide, while plants absorb it

chemicals substances that have a particular composition. Chemical erosion can cause some rocks to wear away. Pollution from human activity can also cause chemicals to leak into soil

continents the continuous expanses of land on Earth. The seven continents are Asia, Africa, North America, South America, Antarctica, Europe, and Oceania

decomposers organisms, such as bacteria and fungi, that help break down organic matter

delta a wetland that forms at the mouth of a river as it empties its water and sediment into the sea, for example

deposited put or set down in a particular area or place

deserts barren landscapes with little rain or snowfall, making it difficult for plants or animals to survive there

droughts prolonged periods of very little rainfall, leading to a shortage of water

ecosystem all the living things in a particular area and the way they interact with each other and with the environment

eruptions violent outbreaks, such as the eruption of molten rock from a volcano

fertile land or soil that is full of nutrients and good for growing crops

fertilizer a chemical or natural substance added to soil to increase its fertility

glaciers slow-moving masses or rivers of ice formed from the accumulation of compacted snow on mountains or near Earth's poles

hibernate to remain inactive for a prolonged period. Many animals hibernate in winter by sleeping or resting

humid when there is a high concentration of water vapor in the air

ice sheets masses of glacial ice more than 19,000 square miles (50,000 sq km) in size

inherit to have qualities or characteristics that are similar to one's parents

insecticides substances used for killing pests or insects that can damage crops

microorganisms microscopic organisms, such as bacteria, fungi, or viruses

minerals substances formed by natural geological processes on Earth. All rocks are made from one or more minerals

nutrients substances that provide nourishment for growth

organic matter carbon-based compounds found in nature that come from the remains of living things, such as plants and animals

pressure a continuous physical force exerted on an object by something it is in contact with. Pressure increases underground, for example, because of the downward push of rock above

protruding sticking out

resource a supply of something that can be used for a particular purpose

Solar System our Sun and the planets and other bodies that orbit it

uplands areas of high or hilly land

weathering the wearing away of a substance over time because of the effects of sunlight, wind, water, or other weather conditions

wetland an area of land that is covered or saturated with water

FIND OUT MORE

Books

DK. *Under Your Feet: Soil, Sand, and Everything Underground.* DK Children, 2020.

Rogers, Marie. *Exploring Weathering and Erosion* (Let's Rock!). Rosen Publishing Group, 2022.

Woolf, Alex. *The Science of Rocks and Minerals: The Hard Truth About the Stuff Beneath Our Feet.* Scholastic, 2018.

Websites

Take another look at the rock cycle at:
www.cotf.edu/ete/modules/msese/earthsysflr/rock.html

Learn more about soil at:
www.soils4kids.org/about

Research more facts about soil at:
www.ducksters.com/science/earth_science/soil_science.php

Publisher's note to educators and parents:
All the websites featured above have been carefully reviewed to ensure that they are suitable for students. However, many websites change often, and we cannot guarantee that a site's future contents will continue to meet our high standards of educational value. Please be advised that students should be closely monitored whenever they access the Internet.

INDEX

ABOUT THE AUTHOR

Sarah Eason has written many books for children on a wide variety of topics, from history to geography and science. She would love to take a rock cycle road trip and visit some of the amazing places explored in this book.